Action Sports

Karate

Bill Gutman

Illustrated with photographs
by Peter Ford

Reading consultant:

John Manning, Professor of Reading
University of Minnesota

Capstone Press
MINNEAPOLIS

Printed in the United States of America.

Capstone Press • 2440 Fernbrook Lane • Minneapolis, MN 55447

Editorial Director   John Coughlan
Managing Editor   John Martin
Copy Editor   Gil Chandler

Library of Congress Cataloging-in-Publication Data

Gutman, Bill.
    Karate / by Bill Gutman.
        p. cm.
    Includes bibliographical references and index.
    ISBN 1-56065-250-0
    1. Karate--Juvenile literature. [1. Karate.]   I. Title.
    GV1114.3.G83   1995
    796.8'153--dc20   94-22963
                                                        CIP
                                                        AC

ISBN: 1-56065-250-0

99 98 97 96 95   8 7 6 5 4 3 2 1

Table of Contents

Chapter 1

The Story of Karate

Karate is a sport and a science. It is a means of self-defense and a great way to stay fit.

With a single blow, a karate expert can kick or punch through a brick or a board. Some can break many bricks or boards at one time. But karate can teach you a lot more than how to break things.

Karate teaches concentration and discipline. It can show you the things your body can do. As an exercise, it builds flexibility, agility, and strength. As a sport, it allows you to test your skill against others.

All karate experts agree that karate should only be used for self-defense. You should never use karate against an untrained person, unless you are attacked. This is a strict code that should always be followed.

A Brief History of Karate

Karate is one of the **martial arts**. Martial arts include all the systems of self-defense that began in Asia. Some other martial arts are judo, aikido, and tae kwon do.

Karate began hundreds of years ago on Okinawa, an island southwest of Japan. Some time around the year 1600, Japanese warriors conquered Okinawa. They issued a law that made it a crime for an Okinawan to own a weapon.

To defend themselves, the Okinawan farmers invented a form of unarmed fighting. Skilled Chinese fighters visited the island to help the Okinawans, who did all their training in secret.

The Okinawans learned about parts of the body that were easy to injure. They toughened

their hands by hitting hard posts and punching sand or gravel. After more than 300 years of this secret self-defense training, their fighting methods came to Japan.

Karate Comes to Japan

In the 1920s, a man named Gichin Funakoshi, a teacher from Okinawa, gave the first demonstration of this self-defense method in Tokyo, the capital of Japan. Funakoshi had been learning the different ways to fight since he was 11 years old. He combined several methods into one style and became the "Father of Karate."

Ginchin Funakoshi also taught that karate should never be used to attack anyone. It should only be used for defense.

Soon after Mr. Funakoshi's visit, Japanese students were taking karate lessons. They learned how to punch and kick. They also learned the many different moves that karate fighters can use. And they worked to improve their strength and stamina.

It would still take more than half a century for karate to become a real sport. There had never been any competitions in Okinawa. Nor were there any at the beginning in Japan.

A Popular Sport in the U.S. and Canada

Karate came to North America in the early 1950s. But it didn't become popular until the 1970s. The movies of Bruce Lee, a karate master, gave the sport a new appeal. Advanced students soon wanted to test their skills. They knew it was wrong to go out and pick a fight. So they organized competitions, and the sport of karate was born.

Chapter 2
Getting Started

A karate student is called a **karate-ka**. A place to learn and practice karate is a **dojo**. Since a karate-ka practices barefoot, dojos have mats on the floor. Most also have mirrors on the walls. Students use the mirrors to watch their form when they practice karate movements, punches, and kicks.

Most karate students wear loose white clothes, including pants and a jacket. A cloth belt ties the jacket at the waist. The color of the belt shows the skill level of the student. Beginning students wear white belts. Later they can earn a yellow, then a green, then a brown belt. You have to pass as many as five tests to earn a green belt, and as many as nine tests to earn the brown belt.

After passing a tenth test, a student can wear the **black belt**. This shows that the student has mastered karate's basic skills and ideas. After earning a black belt, the student may become an instructor and teach karate to others.

It takes two to four years of hard work to earn a first-degree black belt. But the student of karate can go even further–there are 10 degrees of black belts. The more dedication a martial artist has, the higher the **ranking** he or she can earn.

A Sport for Everyone

Anyone can learn karate. Some students are as young as seven years old. Others may be senior citizens. People study karate for the exercise, or they may be interested in competing. Others may want to learn a better way to defend themselves.

A good instructor teaches discipline as well as fighting skills.

No matter how young or old, a new karate student should be in good physical condition. You should try to improve your strength, stamina, and flexibility before you begin karate lessons.

Above, A well-aimed karate kick can break wood or stop an attacker cold. *Right,* Karate is a sport for everyone.

Get in Shape

A few basic exercises can improve your strength. Pushups, situps, and pullups are three good exercises for beginners. They will strengthen your arms, shoulders, and abdominal muscles. Stretching exercises increase flexibility. They usually involve the

legs and groin areas, where it's easy to pull a muscle. Your teacher can show you the best stretching exercises.

Jogging, jumping rope, or biking will improve your stamina. You can also use a treadmill, a stationary bike, or a cross-country skier. These machines will also strengthen your legs. By improving your stamina, you will be able to practice karate without getting tired quickly.

Stretching

Many karate instructors begin their lessons with stretching exercises. These prepare students for the rapid movements and high kicks of karate. If you stretch all the muscles you are going to use, you have less chance of pulling one. A slightly pulled muscle can prevent you from doing some movements. A severely pulled muscle can put you out of action for a long time.

Many instructors also have students stretch and exercise at the end of the lesson.

Chapter 3

Attacking and Blocking

In beginning karate, you learn how to punch or kick your opponent's body. The opponent will try to block your attack. Here are the basic methods of attack and the parts of the opponent's body that are your targets.

The clenched fist. Clench your fingers tightly, with the thumb wrapped around the forefinger and middle finger. To strike the blow, use the spot just below the knuckles of these fingers, or the second joint of the middle finger. The target is usually the opponent's face or one of the softer parts of the body.

The half-clenched fist. Bend the fingers back at the middle joint only. Press the thumb down on the forefinger. Strike with the knuckle of the forefinger or middle finger. The face is the usual target.

The straight hand. Hold the four fingers close together and extend them straight out. Thrust the fingers at the eyes or at the **solar-plexus** (between the chest and stomach). The edge of the hand can also strike with a chopping motion.

The two-finger hand. Extend the forefinger and middle finger straight out. Bend the ring finger and little finger and cover them with the thumb. Use this method for thrusting, usually at the eyes. A single finger is also used to thrust at the eyes.

The target of the clenched fist is usually the face.

Base of the hand. Hold the fingers and thumb together. Point them back and up. The heel of the palm then pushes at the opponent's face, chest, or other areas.

The elbow. Use the elbow to attack the opponent's solar-plexus, chest, or abdomen.

Base of the toes. Turn the toes upward. This takes practice to avoid injury to the toes. Move towards the opponent's body as you kick.

The heel. Use the heel to kick downward or to the rear. If you are being held from the rear, kick the opponent's instep, knee, shin, or groin.

Side of the foot. Turn the toes upward. Move the outside of the foot in a sideways motion. Strike the blow at the knee or at another joint. Again, the wrong motion can injure the toes.

The knee cap is used to strike the groin, stomach, or head.

Knee cap. Use the knee cap to strike at the groin, stomach, or head.

Hammer fist. Make a full clenched fist. Strike the opponent's head or temple with the side of the fist. The motion is like using a hammer.

Blocking an Attack

Here are some basic ways to block the blows described above.

Your forearm can block most attacks. Don't use the soft inside of the forearm, which can easily be injured. Instead, use the sharp edges of the forearm. These are the inner (or thumb-side) edge and the outer (or little finger-side) edge.

When blocking a blow, try to move the attacker's arm away from his or her body. This makes it easier to counterattack. When you have used your arm to block a blow, bring it back quickly. You'll be ready to attack or to block another blow.

The forearm can block even a powerful leg kick.

Blocking Kicks

The ball or edge of the foot can block most kicks. After the block, withdraw your foot immediately. That way, you will recover your balance and be ready to block or attack again. If you block with one hand or foot, you usually counterattack with the other.

You should block punches and kicks as forcefully as you deliver them. This makes blocking more effective. And your opponent will be less likely to attack again.

A fully extended leg delivers the most powerful blow in karate.

Chapter 4

Basic Posture and Movements

There are many moves and counter-moves in karate. Karate students learn how to string these movements together in combinations, called **katas**. Combinations are used for attack and defense.

By practicing kata movements alone, a student can gain speed and skill. They are also a good way to stay fit. Kata movements are like gymnastic routines. They are also an art, like ballet.

The Basic Postures

All karate movements begin with the basic
posture. The body is upright, with the feet
shoulder-width apart. The arms hang relaxed,
with the fists lightly clenched. The hands are
held in front, on each side of the knot in the
middle of the belt.

The second basic posture is similar to the
first. It is used to protect the upper body or to
make counterattacks to the upper body. The
legs and feet are the same as in the basic
posture, but the arms bend upward at the
elbow. The fists are level with the shoulders,
with your palms facing you. Each fist should
be about 12 inches (30 centimeters) from the
shoulder.

Balance and Concentration

When you are learning karate movements,
keep a perfect balance at all times. If you are
steady after a punch or kick, it will be easier to
block your opponent or to mount a second
attack.

Balance by keeping your weight concentrated on the lower part of your body. Always keep your weight centered in the abdominal area and in the legs.

Another important point is concentration. A good karate student always keeps his eyes on the opponent. When practicing, imagine an opponent in front of you. Never look down, whether you're moving upward, downward, or spinning around.

The Straightahead Punch

A basic, straightahead punch in karate is like a left or right jab in boxing. But, unlike a boxer, a karate fighter throws his entire body into the punch.

The blow is delivered while the wrist is twisting and turning. Your thumb points almost upward as you begin. At the moment of impact, the thumb points downward.

Balance and weight should be even. The feet must stay apart and never be placed one behind the other. Your body should remain straight, not lean forward or back.

The arm and clenched fist are thrust straight out in a powerful, compact movement. The lead leg also moves forward, with the knee bent slightly and the foot pointing straight ahead. The rear leg is straight, with the rear foot pointing outward at a 45-degree angle.

If you are going to punch with your left arm, you thrust the left leg and arm forward at the same time. A punch with the right hand is made with the right leg leading. You can also practice a reverse movement, with the right arm punching and the left leg leading, or the left arm punching and the right leg leading.

Practice making these basic punches quickly and powerfully. You can also make one move after another. Learn to go from right to left as quickly as you can. But go slowly. Too much punching can cause an arm injury if your muscles aren't in shape.

Getting Off a Kick

The principles of kicking are the same as punching. The object is to deliver the kick at lightning speed without losing balance. The foot then pulls back just as fast, whether the blow lands or not.

Before the kick, the foot must rise into the kicking position. Bring the knee straight up so the kicking foot is as high as the other knee. This helps you keep your balance. Don't bring the foot back behind the opposite knee.

Flex the knee of the opposite leg slightly. The toes of the kicking foot should bend backward to allow the ball of the foot to make contact. Remember to relax your body, especially the shoulders. A relaxed body develops more power.

Kick by snapping the leg forward at the knee while keeping the body straight. As with the punch, do not lean forward or backward.

In karate, there are many different kicks and punches to learn. But all follow the same rules: relax, concentrate, keep perfect balance, explode with power, withdraw quickly, and be ready for anything.

The Karate Shout

Maybe you have seen karate demonstrations in person or in the movies. There is always a lot of shouting. This is done for a reason. Karate shouts are brought up from the stomach to give you an extra burst of strength when you're attacking or blocking. Your instructor can explain the shout and how it can help you. Shouting will quickly become a part of your karate life.

Chapter 5

Karate Competitions

People study karate for different reasons. Some want to learn how to defend themselves if attacked. Others simply enjoy the exercise or the challenge of learning a complex fighting technique. Many want to see how high a ranking they can reach. Still others want to test themselves against others.

There are many different kinds of karate competitions, including light-contact sport karate, kata competitions, and **full-contact** karate. First make sure you really want to compete. Then choose the kind of competition that best suits you.

Light-Contact Sport Karate

In light-contact sport karate, two contestants **spar** with each other. The object is to score points by completing attack moves. The opponents do not actually strike each other in this form of competition. They must "pull" their punches and kicks just before they land. Some **light contact** is allowed, but a blow that is struck too hard can earn a penalty point.

There are four judges and a referee in light contact. The referee awards points and also takes them away. He also warns competitors who are violating the rules. The four judges assist the referee. They can advise him on a point or on a foul call. Each judge can award one point during a match.

Light-contact karate is a good way to test your moves and your speed against an opponent. Some say this form of karate has too much speed and not enough power, and that it goes against the original object of karate. But light-contact karate is a great way to exercise, work on your moves, and test your skills. And there is little risk of injury.

Kata Contests

A second form of competition is the kata contest. Katas are patterns of attacking and defensive moves. They are done in combinations, like a dance, with a great deal of speed. It takes many hours of practice to get ready for a kata contest. You must work hard to develop a precise, flowing routine.

There are usually four judges who sit at each corner of a large square. Each competitor must announce the kata he will perform before he begins. He will be judged on technique, on the power in his movements, and on how he strikes. The judges also watch timing, form, speed, and even breathing. The competitors must finish at the exact spot where they began. Each performs alone.

Kata contests give karate students a chance to show their athletic ability, as well as their knowledge of the many movements that make up the sport.

Full-Contact Karate

This type of competition is the toughest of all. It has the largest risk of injury and is not for everyone. It is similar to kickboxing, which has become a very popular sport in the 1990's.

Once kickboxing began, several tough karate schools began to hold their own full-contact tournaments. Some allowed protective fist and leg guards, padded gloves, and other footwear. Others allowed no protection at all. As in boxing, points are scored by landing blows.

There are not many full-contact karate matches. They can be dangerous, especially when no protective padding is used. Kickboxing is closely supervised and seems to be the most popular form of full contact. But kickboxing is not pure karate.

A karate student should think very carefully before deciding to try full contact.

Glossary

black belt–a symbol of a karate student's skill level. The black belt means the student has mastered the skills and ideas of karate. Lesser belts are white, yellow, green, and brown.

dojo–a practice gym or any place where karate is taught or practiced

full contact–a form of sport karate in which opponents can hit each other with the full force of their blows

karate-ka–a student of karate

katas–a pattern of karate movements done in rapid succession, one after another. Katas are always performed by a single person.

light contact–a form of sport karate in which the blows are "pulled," or stopped just short of striking an opponent. Only light contact is allowed.

martial arts–the name for the various Asian systems of self-defense. These include karate.

posture–the basic stance a karate-ka takes before attacking or defending himself with karate

ranking–the degree of skill attained by a student of karate. Rankings are shown by the color of the belt a student wears when he is practicing, competing, or receiving a lesson.

solar plexus–the area in the middle of the body just below the chest and above the stomach. The solar plexus is a frequent target of karate blows because it can affect the nerves behind the stomach.

spar–to practice fighting, either with light or full contact

Acknowledgments

Capstone Press wishes to thank Chuck Bainey, Justin Berg, Kristi Broen, Judy Clausen, Jenny Cook, Tom Mueller, Hai Nguyen, Jerry Nguyen, David Smith, and their instructor, Mr. Cristian Nelson, for their help with this project. A special thanks to National Karate Schools for their ongoing cooperation.

To Learn More

Brimner, Larry Dane. *Karate*. New York: Franklin Watts, 1988.

Leder, Jane Mersky. *Karate*. Marco, FL: Bancroft-Sage, 1992.

Neff, Fred. *Karate is for Me*. Minneapolis: Lerner Publications, 1980.

Queen, J. Allen. *Complete Karate*. New York: Sterling, 1992.

Sipe, Dan. *Kickboxing*. Minneapolis: Capstone Press, 1994.

Some Useful Addresses

National Karate Association of Canada
220 1367 West Broadway
Vancouver, BC V6M 4A9

U.S.A. Karate Federation
1300 Kenmore Road
Akron, OH 44314

U.S.A.-Korean Karate Association
P.O. Box 1401
Great Falls, MT 59403-1401

Index